Live Like a Toddler

Be the Young Explorer of Your Life

Tatiana Wells

Copyright © 2017 Tatiana Wells

All rights reserved.

All Bible scriptures used in this book are from the New King James Version (NKJV) and the Message (MSG).

ISBN: 0692963464
ISBN-13: 978-0692963463

This book is dedicated to all the parents who allowed me to educate and care for their children and to the children who inspired me to live each day daringly with great expectation. And to all my family, friends, and mentors—my push-and-pull people—who accepted my toddler-like behavior and encouraged me to complete this project.

CONTENTS

	Introduction	i
1	Curious	7
2	Know That *No* Means *NO*	13
3	Independently Dependent	21
4	Time for a Temper Tantrum	30
5	Exploration Try	40
6	Use Large Paper and Crayons	49
7	Importance of Play	54
8	Whom are you Mimicking?	64
9	Go Ahead: I Dare You to *Jump!*	69
	Toddler Living Tips	82
	References	92
	Scripture References	94

INTRODUCTION

Young Explorers

Toddlers rule! Ask anyone about a toddler, and you'll likely hear "terrible twos" in response because the once-cute infant has become an independent explorer who is testing his or her limits. Education theorist Jean Piaget (Taylor 2008, 269) describes this stage as the preoperational phase, in which the world centers on the child: the child calls the shots and is not bothered by other people's points of view. Toddlers are solely focused on their own needs, wants, and desires, unconcerned with how frustrated with, tired of, or discontented by their actions their caregivers may be.

Sitting at an overcrowded round table at yet another boring conference, I scanned the room and noticed all the well-behaved adults dressed in their boring black-and-white business suits, dresses, or pants and cardigans. We all sat properly, surrounded by coffee cups, saucers, plates, goblets, silverware, and of course, the floral centerpieces. I immediately thought of my favorite students, the busy toddlers. I imagined that if toddlers were sitting at the table, they would have made music with the forks and plates, tasted the butter that looked like whipped cream, crawled on the floor to play peekaboo, or had temper tantrums by now. They would want to be released from their parents' laps to practice running through the big conference room in the hope that someone would chase them. I wished I were a toddler instead of an adult in that moment. I whispered this scene to a colleague who was sitting with me, and she laughed in agreement. Our snickering intrigued our tablemates, who were curious about the content of our more interesting conversation. They obliged by adding additional details to the scenario, and more chuckling and acting out erupted. We had become the noisy table; we received glares from the well-behaved adults who were trying to listen to the monotonous woman talk about how to be more courageous. And from there, the concept of living like a toddler was born.

Henceforth, I applied the toddler point of view in my everyday situations. Dictionary.com defines a toddler as "a person who toddles, especially a young child learning to walk." When toddlers learn to walk, they flail their arms like baby birds trying out their wings, their little legs wobble for balance, and they look as if they're holding their breath, getting ready for takeoff. As adults, we sometimes forget our first-time emotions when we start something new. When I hear adults talk about new adventures, such as returning to school or starting their own businesses, they express their fears and worries more than the excitement and courage of the opportunity to have new beginnings. We overlook the joy and exhilaration that accompany novel ideas. But to start a new adventure is breathtaking!

Taking our first steps toward a new job may cause our legs to wobble. Asking someone out on a date can cause butterflies. And yes, there is a possibility of falling, but just as we encourage toddlers to let go of our fingers to walk on their own, we have to be ready to toddle. *On your mark. Get set. Go!*

When was the last time you dared yourself to step outside your comfort zone? Complacency is robotic; it involves the same moves, the same conversation, and the same routine lifestyle of coming and going. In toddler classrooms, children are encouraged to move liberally throughout the room. Teachers guide them to new toys and provide supplemental materials to keep them engaged. The toddlers are viewed as young explorers because they touch, taste, see, smell, and hear everything—which is why parents usually tiptoe around them when they're sleeping. They hide in small places; run in big spaces; and jump, flip, and roll everywhere, and they are known to randomly walk out of rooms to explore different surroundings. They usually wear bright, bold colors and large prints. The girls love tutus, and the boys love their dinosaur rain boots. Ironically, when they grow up, their curiosity wanes, and they become well-behaved adults who attend conferences in nicely fitted, matching clothes with just a pop of color on a tie or a purse to add some fashion flair.

Dare to think outside the adult box. Like toddlers eager to explore their world, let's be prepared to ignite our passions, spark our subconscious minds to consciousness, and step into new territory outside our comfort zones.

1 Curious

From infancy, children innately observe their surroundings. At first they have limited opportunities to tangibly experience their environments because they are held either in caregivers' arms or in holding devices like car seats or bouncers. And of course they are unable to walk or crawl to desired objects. For several months to a little over a year, children's eyes capture the colorful hues of shiny, odd-shaped objects, but their minds can only long to discover their textures and purposes.

Infants use their vision to prepare their

hands to grasp the objects they see (McCarty et al. 2001, 973). I'm sure many parents can attest to this statement as they reminisce about how their infants grabbed their necklaces, chains, hair, or earrings and refused to let go. Infants' parents have constantly but unknowingly been enticing them with items full of colorful beads, feathers, and shiny gold while leaning over to change diapers and tickle and play with their lovable children. While parents laugh and play with their babies, the babies are trying to send command signals to their tactile senses to grab the fascinating objects.

My toddler expertise was developed in my former position as a childcare director. To live your life like a toddler, you must develop the curiosity to find out how things work. Focus your eyes on something tangible, and reach for it. As adults, we rely on our experience rather than applying

> *To live your life like a toddler, you must develop the curiosity to find out how things work.*

imagination. We become jaded, in a sense. But we don't know everything nor have we experienced it all. There is an entire world that consists of seven continents and five oceans. In the United States alone, there are fifty states, five Great Lakes, and thousands of cities to discover. It is possible for anyone to learn something new every day. Curiosity causes thinkers to fashion what was once considered impossible, entrepreneurs to expand, and artists to create masterpieces.

Reminded of the two-year-olds who visited my office after running an errand with their teacher, I recall their curious behavior when they visited me in the office. They ran in and greeted me with hugs—their expressions of affection were sweet but also small, manipulative ploys to get the teacher to talk to me as they inquisitively explored any drawer, button, desk object, or other item they could reach and touch. Questions and commands quickly interrupted the conversation between the teacher and me.

"What's this, Tati-nana?"

"What chu doing that for?"

"Can I do that?"

"Stop."

"Don't touch that."

"Thank you."

"No."

"Uh-oh!"

"Bring me that, please."

After a five-minute chat, the teacher tried to gather the children and have them clean up the hurricane of a mess they had made through their exploratory behavior.

Is there something you have had your eye on for some time now? Are you curious about another part of town or a country that you would like to travel to? What's holding you back? You hold the key to your destiny, and curiosity is the ignition—maybe this should be your very own mantra. I hear children, especially teenagers, often say, "I can't wait to become an adult so I can do what I want." You already are an adult and can make things happen. Find something that interests you. It could be work, a hobby, or a getaway. It could include your family or spouse, or better yet, just as a toddler would think, it could be something just for you. Ignite your curiosity today by taking a time-out moment to reflect on your behavior, your thoughts, your past dreams, and your desires. Think about the things you said you wanted to do when you were in high school or college—or just last week. Why continue to put off for tomorrow things that can be done today? Yes, apply to school, write that grant to start your own business, visit your friend across the world or town, or take that dance class. The world is waiting for you to fulfill your destiny and bring it something better—a new, more experienced you.

Toddler Living Tip:

- **Create expeditions out of normality.** In your normal daily tasks, take a moment to ask yourself, "What do I really want to do and why haven't I done it yet?" Each day try to explore something new such as taking a different route to work, eating at a new restaurant for lunch, or visiting a place you have wondered about for the past few months. This is your moment to explore your surroundings. When you travel to a new city or country, plan to have a new experience, such as cooking, dancing, swimming, or sightseeing, or even jump into a big sink hole. Don't just visit familiar places and eat at the same restaurants that you have in your town; explore something new.

- **Ask questions.** I hear educators say, you can always tell a person's intelligence by the questions they ask. Toddlers are known for asking "why" all the time. Instead of just accepting the status quo, inquire how to change your circumstances. You are a child of God and do not have to settle for mediocrity.

2 Know That *No* Means *NO*

If you were to ask the parent of a toddler to say a common word that his or her child says, one of the top five responses would probably be *no*. As spirited infants transition into the toddler stage, they are on exploratory missions to do everything they have seen the tall people around them do. Their mission is to run, touch, examine, and be rulers of themselves. Unfortunately for them, their caregivers will not allow them to accomplish these tasks without using the reinforcing word *no* almost a million times before their second and third birthdays;

therefore the word *no* becomes associated with the power to control, and it becomes the most used word for the egocentric child.

The word *no* is a mighty word of authority; it is so powerful that some adults hesitate to move forward because of the fear of hearing this word. Isn't that the reason you haven't applied for that new position, asked the object of your affections out on a date, or asked for a raise? Parents use this word with toddlers to protect them from harming themselves, but the toddlers use the word liberally and literally to say, "I'm in control of this situation." A toddler's *no*, however, has no connection with the emotions of the other person, which means that he or she won't say yes to eating vegetables or using the potty just to appease Mommy or Daddy.

When I observed my toddlers, I loved seeing their interactions with one another during exploratory learning. I like to call a toddler classroom a training ground because that's where toddlers learn the essential daily functions of social relations—how to walk, talk, and relate to others.

As the children played with toys in their small groups, I would observe a child attempting to take a toy away from another child. Immediately the teacher would intervene to teach the child that, per societal norms, we must ask for what we want and not snatch it away from our friends. She would coach the child to ask the friend to play with the toy, and I'd smile when the friend would respond with a simple, unemotional *no*. Another behavior I noticed in this dynamic of assertiveness was that if the first child cried when the friend refused to share, the friend would simply look at the child, unaffected by his or her emotions.

The egocentric nature of this interaction falls into Piaget's preoperational stage. Toddlers do not have a sense of other people's feelings. Again, the toy's "owner" was concerned not with the friend's feelings but only with his or her own simple unwillingness to share. The teacher would then redirect the other child to another toy. But the most amazing thing that I observed when this occurred was the child's application of a concrete thought to care for another person. The redirected child did not have a tantrum; he or she simply played with the other toy. And the other child, once finished with the first toy, took the toy to his or her friend. We all celebrated when this happened.

Some people in your life may ask you for your belongings all the time, especially if you are a parent. They may give you those puppy dog eyes, a sad story of urgency, or some manipulation that involves your supposed guilt. No matter which tactic they use, it's OK to decline. As a leader, mentor, sister, and daughter, I also had to learn the tactic of saying no when my employees, friends, and family members presented requests that would probably have benefited them more than me. Most times I would abandon my pre-planned scheduled or adjust my finances to meet their needs. Although saying no is hard, I learned to disassociate myself from feelings of guilt when I had to reject my these appeals. As toddlers had taught me, it was not about the people's emotions. It was the principle of the thing. *No* means *no*.

As a former childcare director, I recall many encounters with persons twenty-four to thirty-six inches tall screaming *no* at moments of transition—returning to the classroom after playing outside on a warm day, putting shoes back on, or lying down for nap time. They were not considerate of how tired the teachers or I were, nor did the fact that we were in charge of twelve other toddlers make a difference to them. During those moments, we as caregivers had to know that *no*—their *no*—meant *no*.

To whom or what do you need to express the "unemotional *no*" in your life? Is it that relative who calls every three months before getting evicted? Does a spouse or partner constantly ask you to do something because the person knows you'll say yes? Do you take on additional assignments that hinder your productivity instead of increasing it? We make too many excuses for why we can't ask for what we want. Women especially put the needs of others, like family members, before their own, and in doing so, they silently murder their true passions and desires.

Remember that on an airplane, the attendant reminds you, in the case of an emergency, to put your oxygen mask on first before helping someone else. The purpose of this advisory is to remind you that if you're hurt, you can't help anyone else. Learn to use these two letters, *n-o*, to save yourself. Know your limits; remember that portion control is necessary for balance. No matter the situation, be like a toddler and assertively take your new stand on *no*. Rejecting a lot of additional tasks will bring you freedom in other areas in your life. No is a sentence that doesn't always require an explanation. Practice it and see how liberating and in control you feel, but be careful using no with your boss.

> *Remember that portion control is necessary for balance.*

Toddler Living Tips:

- **No is a sentence.** One year my mom told us that during the week of Thanksgiving she was practicing using the word no. Her birthday usually falls during that holiday week, therefore she gave her disclaimer in advance that she would be using her authoritative no. And as the cooking and clean up chores came about, when we asked mom to help she smiled while simply using her one word sentence, "*no*". You'll be surprised how liberating it is to say no and how much time you regain when kindly declining someone's request. And remember no is a sentence; there's no explanation needed.
- **Be steadfast and unmovable.** The Bible says in 1 Corinthians 15:58 MSG, "With all this going for us, my dear, dear friends, stand your ground. And don't hold back. Throw yourselves into the work of the Master, confident that nothing you do for him is a waste of time or effort." Toddlers are very confident in their decisions. This is the reason you see little girls wearing princess dresses and mixed match

shoes and boys wearing pillowcases as their superhero capes in the grocery stores because they won the fight with their parents to dress in their favorite outfits. Practice assertiveness and confidence in your decisions, and try to avoid arrogance.

- **Do something different from what you are asked to do.** Have you ever witnessed someone tell a toddler to do something and they immediately respond with no and do the opposite thing they were instructed not to do? For example, a parent tells the child to stop running and they keep running, or the parent asks the child to kiss them and the child turns their head. I always appreciated my staff who would exceed my expectations by enhancing the directive I gave them. Dare to go beyond other people's expectations of you. Surprise them by exerting extra effort to do things a little differently. Remember that raises and promotions are often given to those who take initiative to enhance their work performance.

3 Independently Dependent

I thought of calling this chapter "The Test." The test would come when I sat with one of my darling toddlers and documented whether the child had mastered an essential developmental skill—fine or gross motor, cognitive, or social—by having the child complete a relevant task. When administering a developmental screening, it's best to do so in a natural setting where the child is comfortable and does not know that a test is happening. One of the many things I liked to observe was children's introduction to jigsaw puzzles.

Eagerly pouring pieces onto a table and

putting them back in place seems very simple to the little ones, but their thinking processes begin when they realize that the pieces need to be twisted, flipped, and arranged correctly to fit. Based on his or her personality, a child may either immediately ask for help or be a Mr. or Miss Independent. The children who yearned for their independence as they attempted to complete the task on their own staged mini-tantrums when I tried to help. They struggled with the pieces, became frustrated, and sometimes even walked away.

Another test was simultaneously taking place. This test was the one within me as the caregiver, nurturer, and teacher. I wanted to help as the child struggled. I wanted to eliminate the child's stress, disappointment, and frustration. I watched, knowing that children at this tender age typically figure this one out on their own. Then I smiled as the child pushed my hand away when I gave in to the temptation to help, and I smiled again when the child put a puzzle piece in my hand, thereby asking me to help.

Toddlers so desire to be independent, but due to their limited knowledge and ability, they are naturally dependent upon help from grown-ups.

Can you see the picture? If you are a parent, I'm sure this sounds very familiar. I like to think of the players in this scenario as children of God. How often do we manipulate, twist, and struggle with the puzzle pieces of our lives when we are put into situations that we believe we can handle on our own? I believe that at these moments God has come to test our maturity. Perhaps you've been presented the opportunity to complete a major project at work. You may approach the situation fully excited, believing that you can achieve anything, but right away you find yourself making your "test" longer and harder. You try to flip the situation. You manipulate the pieces to fit your mold. And when others ask you if you need help, you answer with much pride, "No, thank you" (because now you use your assertive *no*).

All the while our Father sits in heaven,

thinking, "I wish [he or she] would just ask me for help; I'm waiting." I believe He yearns to help us and shakes His head as we spin and flip the pieces around, trying to do it on our own. Jeremiah 33:3, MSG urges us to seek help:

> Call to me, and I will answer you. I'll tell you marvelous and wondrous things that you could never figure out on your own.

Or James 1:5–8 MSG says this:

> If you don't know what you're doing, pray to the Father. He loves to help. You'll get his help, and won't be condescended to when you ask for it.

Our gracious God knows that when we run to the end of ourselves, we will call upon Him, and faithful as He is, He will respond and direct our paths.

All skill tests for toddlers are given on numerous occasions until the skills are mastered. Some toddlers walk away after a few minutes of not being able to complete the puzzle; others keep at it, even if it means asking for help. The teachers celebrate on the day when a child who initially struggled grabs the puzzle, sits down, completes the puzzle independently, and then runs to them, saying, "I did it!" Isn't this what our Father in heaven longs for as well? He gives us a job to do; it may be ministry, the marketplace in your community or workplace, parenting, or something else. And though challenging along the way, it builds our faith and patience. It builds our confidence. For it is written thus:

> My brethren, count it all joy when you fall into various trials, knowing that the testing of your faith produces patience. But let patience have its perfect work, that you may be perfect and complete, lacking nothing.
> (James 1:2–4 NKJV)

I remember another occasion of observing a child as he excitedly told me he could button his shirt. I anxiously watched the child make multiple attempts to button the three buttons on his polo shirt. By the second button, eight minutes later, I tried to help the child, but he pushed my hands away and said, "No, no, I can do it myself!" And finally, after another five minutes, he successfully finished buttoning his shirt and proclaimed, "I told you I could do it." To my chagrin, he had buttoned his shirt lopsided.

I learned a variety of lessons in this particular instance. From my perspective—that of the person who is always trying to help someone—sometimes "help" can be a hindrance. Though the child buttoned the shirt lopsided, the task he mastered was buttoning; the next time he would concentrate on matching button and buttonhole evenly. When we lend our helping hands, sometimes we interfere with the learning process, debilitating the learner's independence and fostering codependence. Over helping has also been called the "God complex"; my pastor calls it the "Holy Ghost Jr." position. Parents run behind their children with pillows to soften their falls; friends bail their friends out even if the friends don't ask for help; loved ones enable one another and pray that they will become independent.

As a manager in my twenties, I was often given the liberty to run my department independently as I saw fit. There were moments when I thought my supervisor was crazy for trusting me with such an enormous task; I would quickly become frustrated when it seemed to be too much. But every time I pushed forth, I became a stronger, more confident, and smarter manager.

Parents of young adult children, remember that trials may come upon your kids, but you cannot be so quick to answer or fix their problems, for their tests will produce maturity. And that's exactly what you pray for. To the businessperson who is faced with the many challenges of operating an organization, "let patience

> *"Let patience have its perfect work, that you may be perfect and complete, lacking nothing" (James 1:4 NKJV).*

have its perfect work, that you may be perfect and complete, lacking nothing" (James 1:4 NKJV). For the student who is struggling in school, keep trying and never give up, for your help is just a prayer away. Continue to push through, "for the Spirit in you is far greater than anything in this world" (1 John 4:4 MSG). Remember that your test is coming, but God is right there watching you and wanting to help you as much as you want Him to. Be patient for the answer as your faith muscles develop and patience has its perfect work. Independence is good and necessary, but it does not eliminate all need to ask for help. And remember, God's help comes in different forms, such as a coworker, an employee, a child, a parent, or a pastor. In biblical times, God even used a donkey to give a message. You can do all things through Christ who strengthens you.

Toddler Living Tips:

- **Exercise your independence.**

During this stage, toddlers learn to dress themselves, zip a zipper, and manipulate figures. Just as they learn new skills, you can learn something new, like dance, a new language, or how to pay your own bills.

- **Feed yourself.** If you attend church, this is a great time for you to learn how to encourage yourself. Although your pastors and church leaders are there for you, you have to start feeding yourself with the Word of God to increase your faith muscles.

4 Time For A Temper Tantrum

Tantrums are common in early childhood (Beldan, Thomson, and Luby 2008, 117). Common tantrum behaviors, such as crying and hitting, can occur at least once a day and last between one and five minutes. Temper tantrums are an expected and normal part of development. Yes, this statement is true. Children ages eighteen to 36 months are usually referred to as being in "the terrible twos" due to their obnoxious but *normal* temper tantrum behavior. Temper tantrums at this age are usually associated with toddlers' limited vocabulary, inability to get access to something they truly desire, inability to retrieve something that someone has taken away, or fatigue. Their demonstrative expressions can be overwhelming, but as the caregiver, you learn to handle the situation by figuring out what they are attempting to communicate and either getting them what they want or turning the moment into a teachable one. Most times you'll see adults rushing to get the children what they want quickly, just to end the fuss.

Toddlers also throw tantrums because, as discussed in the previous chapter, they are independently dependent. Though they get excited about accomplishing so many new things, they become very frustrated when they come up against something they can't master. And as I've stated, they don't always want to ask for help from the adult in charge.

Remember that tantrums are called a "normal part of development," and adults have them too. What new task have you attempted and failed at? Think about what happened when you tried to download a new program on your computer, assemble a new shelf with limited instructions, install a sump pump to keep your basement from flooding before the next big storm, or correct a billing situation when you couldn't find the right terms to describe the problem. What happened on your family vacation when your husband or wife constantly directed you as to how to drive, even though you've been driving since you were fourteen years old? Did you say a few swear words, throw something, or yell or grunt? Did you want to call for help, or did you have the deep desire to do the task yourself?

When toddlers perform tantrums well enough, adults usually rush to get them what they want. The caregiver even learns how to prevent future outbursts by implementing different strategies to prevent failure, frustration, and miscommunication for the child. Some may also take the opportunity to teach the child how to communicate

> *A tantrum causes someone to react to your need with a solution.*

effectively. In essence, a tantrum causes someone to react to your need with a solution.

When was the last time you had a temper tantrum that caused someone else to act? Some of us had nice caretakers who taught us that we don't show our emotions or cry out loud when we want something but should quietly ask and wait for what we want. Toddlers abandon this rule—and often. If they want something, they go after it, and when they can't get it, they scream, kick, throw things, or cry, and they do so loudly. And they do this not only in the privacy of their homes but also in the company of others in public places, no matter the time of day. They cause others—and sometimes themselves—to take action right away.

Have you looked at your bank account lately? Are you still working for the same agency where you put in 200 percent of your energy and time, have excellent annual reviews, and may even be the most valuable employee, but management has refused to give you a raise for yet another year? Have you been overlooked for a position you desired? Well, did you have a temper tantrum about it or just whine to your friends and family? A child's whine is a very annoying sound that adults either ignore or try to stifle. But no one can ignore a tantrum.

So let's hone your temper tantrum skills to fit your adult status. Go after that promotion hard, and if management still rejects your request, write an impressive letter expressing why you deserve that promotion. I know someone who interviewed with a company and was told she had an excellent interview and references but not enough experience for the job. Disappointed by the news, because she believed from her stellar interview and rapport with the interviewing staff that she had earned the position, she did not settle for that comment. She made a rebuttal. She tactfully thanked the company for taking the time to interview her, but she didn't stop there. She called the interviewer again to advocate for herself and boasted about her acquired skills and ability to learn fast.

Now some may say her demonstrative expression was arrogant. But why did this conversation lead to another phone call from the company, this one telling her that the staff was working on the details of her contract to meet all of her requests because she was still being considered for the position? She had a tantrum. She loudly communicated her point and was heard, causing someone to create a solution by tending to her needs. When are *you* going to have a temper tantrum?

Some of us need to have temper tantrums with ourselves, for starters, to straighten out finances that are in ruins, walk out of a toxic relationship, or apply for a new job and leave an unproductive and unfruitful place. I hope that when you read this, you become uncomfortable in your nest. It's time to go hard after your true desires! Don't make excuses; just go for results. Shout for what you want, go after it with zeal, and don't stop kicking and screaming until you get it. Remember that the best tantrums cause others to rush to get you what you want. If no one is coming to you with the desired resolution, then you're probably not having a tantrum but just whining instead, and whining gets ignored. This process is even easier when you can articulate your words well enough during your kicking and screaming to get what you want.

You've told God that you want a Ford Escape, yet in your heart, you want a Mercedes-Benz GLK 350. Yeah, that's what I did. I told God I wanted an Escape just because my thinking focused on what I deserved in my young thirties, and I thought He could bless me with my sincere desire for a Mercedes when I got older and more accomplished. Well, that's not scriptural, for the Bible says in Psalm 37:4–5 NKJV, "Delight yourself in the Lord, that He will give you the desires of your heart." As a faithful friend of God, I was in the right position, age, time, and opportunity for Him to bless me with my real request. And after almost not receiving this blessing, I went to my Heavenly Father and had my temper tantrum by commanding my blessing reminding God of His words that He said I can have what I ask for if I believe. So I went visiting multiple Mercedes Benz dealers making my request known, and within a week and two days after Christmas, I got my new Mercedes-Benz GLK 350 for an unbelievable price. It even had a few extra features I hadn't asked for, causing me to remember that God blesses above our expectations. And it was $200 cheaper than the Ford Escape! I also imagine a tantrum when I think of Matthew 7:7 NKJV, which says, "Ask, and it will be given unto you; seek, and you will find; knock, and the door will be opened." Some of you are giving up on your desires too soon. If you only ask and walk away, you can miss God's answer to bless you. It's time to stop and make a demonstrative expression.

Have you ever heard a parent yell, "Just give them what they want already"? Remember, tantrums are normal and used to get what we want. That unfulfilled desire within you is anxiously waiting for you to thrust yourself forward, have a tantrum, and finally get what you want. The next time you're going to the car dealership, preparing for your annual evaluation, or going boldly before the Father, remember it's OK to have a temper tantrum — to demonstratively express yourself to get what you want. When you do this appropriately, others will rush to make sure you are satisfied.

Toddler Living Tips:

- **Be aggressive and take it by force.** When toddlers have a temper tantrum because someone took away their toy, they are known to grab the toy back from the person who took it from them. What has the enemy stolen from you? Get upset and go get your stuff! "For the kingdom suffers violence, and the violent take it by force" Matthew 11:12 NKJV.
- **Become frustrated when things don't go your way.** Go hard after what you want, whether it's a date, partner, job, car, home, or promotion. Make something happen; don't settle.

- **Learn how to throw and kick.** Find out how to throw away things that you don't need and that are holding you back. Kick out all of those negative things, people, and habits that hinder your development.
- **Ask for items by name.** Be specific in your requests to receive the true desires of your heart.

5 Exploration Try

> *The toddler, through imagination, can quickly transform their ideas of what the play space represents in terms of changing the optical (real) field to the sense (imaginary) field. This means that a toddler can simultaneously be inside and outside the fields of their real or imagined play space (Li, Quinones, & Ridgway 2016, 65).*

Anyone who babysits a toddler will tell you that toddlers move regularly and staying still is not an option. Toddlers are young explorers seeking all they can acquire. They enjoy learning new skills, and they learn them by doing them, actively engaging in the activity at hand. Just allow a little person to roam in the kitchen freely, and she will open and close the cabinet drawers multiple times, remove pots and pans, climb into cupboards to play hide-and-seek, and open the refrigerator to find something she can put in her mouth. Toddlers use all five senses of seeing, touching, smelling, hearing, and tasting to learn how to interact with and manipulate new discoveries. Toddlers love trying new things. They are attracted to objects because of their novelty. Educators and pediatricians strongly encourage parents to have their youngsters try new things, new foods, and new games and meet new friends. When was the last time you ventured from your norms to explore something new?

Though routines help build trust, security, and confidence in our lives, we as adults use routines as a default, and in this way, we disable flexibility. A myth claims, "Humans use only 10 percent of their brains." Has the myth derived from the notion that humans fail to exercise the power of their minds beyond their daily routines?

Our brains continually develop from birth throughout adulthood. The plasticity of our brains allows for growth and development with each new encounter. While some people can drive a route in their city from memory, taking a different route each day causes the neurons in the brain to fire or communicate across other synapses and causes the brain to work more efficiently to recognize and apply the new routes. It's like exercising any other muscle; it may seem as if two-minute planks or fifty crunches are impossible when you first begin, but after you repeat the task for endurance, the workout becomes possible. Like Adam, who was given the job to name every creature on earth, we, too, can use our creative genius to think of the incredible possibilities. Can you imagine the potential of our minds? Some people believe that geniuses with intelligence quotients of 140 or higher are the only ones able to create something original, but toddlers do it all the time. They look at objects through a different lens. They explore everything they sense. For example, when you feed toddlers, they often spit out the food placed in their mouths because they want to study the texture, taste, and smell of the food. Sheets turn into superhero capes, tiaras transform little girls into princesses of magical forests, and swords make young boys become warriors and knights. It's during these magic years that children learn how to think and believe the impossible. As they grow older, they reach the age of reasoning, at which point they realize they cannot fly and trade their princess dresses and superhero capes for cell phones and tablets. Hold on to your imagination and explore something new. What was the last thing you explored?

Toddlers try new things is said to promote balance and control. When stuck in a routine, we become one-sided and lose our balance. Have you read that Americans are overworked? Americans have a workaholic culture that measures success by the amount of work someone does.

Our society enforces long work hours, extremely busy schedules, and constant motion. Recall that iconic New York City is referred to as "the city that never sleeps." We box ourselves into these daily schedules, which cause stress and multiple mental health issues. Parents even fill their children's calendars with activities. Our elder generations established the trend of the noble deed of finding a "good job" with "good benefits," and they worked that angle until they retired in their sixties. But our latest generation is different; my eleven-year-old niece tells me she's going to be a deep-sea diver, farmer, and veterinarian, and she has the tenacity to fulfill all three dreams. I don't discourage her because she's tapping into multiple talents and God given ability rather than perfecting just one. She's applying what educational theorist Howard Gardner calls *multiple intelligences* (Leshkovska and Spaseva 2016, 58). Gardner proved that there are eight intelligences: linguistic, spatial, visual, musical, kinesthetic, interpersonal, intrapersonal, and natural. Someone who may not have the ability to construct things without directions could be a very talented musician and a great poet. To distinguish our talents, we have to use them and try new things. It's time to explore some new sights, new destinations, and new ideas. Try something new! Go ahead; you can do it. Move beyond your comfort zone, push past the default button, and look within yourself to discover a new talent.

Building a new skill allows you to progress from your foundation. You've earned the degree; you have multiple years of experience and expertise under your belt. Now is the time to share this knowledge in a different form (possibly as a manager or supervisor), establish a new business, or conduct some trainings. Create something new! It's your time to apply for that higher position that you've secretly desired. Or maybe you're someone like one of my former teaching-staff members, who enjoyed working with children and did it very well but dreamed of doing something completely different. Her real passion was becoming a cosmetologist. Luckily for the little girl who walked into her classroom with her hair undone, the teacher fulfilled her true passion and gave that child a hairdo makeover. Not only did the little girl smile, but I noticed how much joy the teacher expressed, too. She was one of my best teachers, among other great staff members, but when the opportunity came for me to encourage her to return to school to pursue a child-development certificate or degree, I could not bring myself to encourage her to continue to follow an undesired path. Instead I called her into my office to tell her that I would terminate her employment before I asked her to go to school for something she was good at but was not passionate about. And on that day, we called hair schools instead of reviewing early-childhood courses. By the end of that year, we released her, and the next month, she was enrolled in cosmetology school full-time. Today, she is overbooked with clients young and elderly, and it's all because she tried something out of her comfort zone. Doing something because you're good at it is different from doing something that you love. Some people treat their passions as hobbies instead of applying their talents to employment opportunities. The former teacher now makes more money as a cosmetologist than she did as a teacher.

As a child, I loved dancing. Whenever music came on, my mom would call me to dance for the family. I also participated in multiple talent shows. Though I didn't have any formal training, my passion for dance never subsided—not even when I became saved. God just put my dance talent to His use. I loved praise dancing and had always wanted to take part, but now, in my thirties, I was afraid to try something new. But I pushed past the fear and contacted a praise-dance instructor to ask if I could attend her practices. Within one year, I started dancing at my church, and a couple of years later, I had the opportunity to perform in a large production with a local dance company.

It's never too late to try something new. Anyone who loves to cook for others should put on a make-believe chef hat and apron and try a small catering business or a restaurant pop-up. Those who always wanted to be doctors should remember that there is no age limit for returning to school. Go for it! If you need a visual, put on your house robe to pretend it's a white medical coat and see yourself in the position. Everyone should plan to do something different, whether it's leaving work earlier; traveling to a new part of town, a new city, or another country; or as my friends urge me to do all the time, ordering something new on the menu. There are limitless possibilities in this world. No matter your age or ability level, you haven't tested them all, so go ahead: live like a toddler and open the door to new possibilities. Use your natural toddler senses and explore it all.

Toddler Living Tip:

Try new things. Doctors often advise parents to allow their toddlers to try new foods, toys, and places. My advice to you is the same. Venture out of your comfort zone. New opportunities don't usually knock on your door; you have to seek new activities, new jobs, new friends, and even new talents. Pick up a pencil to draw something; you might discover that you are an artist.

6 Use Large Paper And Crayons

"Who wants to color?" yells the toddler teacher who's prepping the playroom with huge sheets of bulletin board paper and fat crayons for the children to use. Toddlers love to make marks on paper, tables, and walls. Unlike older children, they do not care about coloring inside the lines. In a childcare setting, it is prohibited to use printed-out coloring sheets for this age group. Toddlers are encouraged to create their art. Likewise, it's time for you to create your masterpiece, your Sistine Chapel frescoes, your *Mona Lisa*.

Here's your chance to "write the vision

and make it plain on tablets" (Habakkuk 2:2 NKJV). Take a moment to envision yourself embarking upon something challenging, rewarding, and fun. Grab a big sheet of paper and draw your idea.

> *Take a moment to envision yourself embarking upon something challenging, rewarding, and fun.*

Dream big! There is no vision too big or insignificant for God. If you think you're not the best artist, then contact a printing company to help you design your plan. On the World Wide Web, you will find all kinds of resources — articles called "How to Start a Business" or "How to Draw Up a Business Plan," for example, along with other ideas you may need to enhance your vision. Make vision boards using magazine clippings, pictures, and articles. And these days, there's always an app at your fingertips. Remember from chapter 1 that infants focus their eyes on an object and then grasp it. If you have to see it to believe it, make sure you look at these boards, plans, apps, and mission statements every day — and grab them!

I love children's art because, though it starts as only a few slanted, colorful lines, when you step back and look at what was freely created, it's always interesting. There's more to the picture than just simple lines drawn; there is an image made. As our students finished drawing, we would ask them what they had drawn. I loved hearing their formative minds go to work as they shared, with their limited vocabularies, all that they saw as I wrote their words on the paper. What was most enchanting about their naming their art was that the images would become apparent to me, too! I could see what they were describing. Though at first glance, their work looked like swirls, circles, and scribbles, I soon saw the cars emerging from the circles, dragons eating the trees, and funny cartoon characters coming to life on the page. The same will happen for you. Write your vision so that others can see it.

Psychologists use a personality test called the House-Tree-Person (HTP) test, developed by John Buck, as a tool to obtain further data on personality traits of adults and children, an extension of the Goodenough Scale (Niolon 2003). Administration of the HTP requires three sheets of copy paper, with instructions for the person to draw a house on one sheet, a tree on the second sheet, and a person on the third sheet. The test is also useful with speech-handicapped patients. Buck interpreted the drawings as unconscious reflections of each test taker's personality (Niolon 2003). For example, the size of the drawing of the person (P) would correspond to the real person's unconscious feelings about himself or herself. So when you draw your vision, think of yourself already successful because that's who God created you to be.

I repeat, take heed of Habakkuk 2:2–3 MSG: "It aches for the coming—it can hardly wait! If it seems slow in coming, wait. It's on its way. It will come right on time. Write out in big bold letters so you can read it and run with it. This vision-message is a witness pointing to what's coming."

Toddler Living Tips:

- **Make marks with crayon on paper or the table.** Make some marks to create your vision. Set aside time to envision the big dream. You don't have to wait to retire or earn more money; plan your future today. Why put off things until tomorrow? Have an arts and crafts day, a business-writing day, or a vision board day. "He encourages us that He will do exceedingly, abundantly, above what we ask or think" (Ephesians 3:20 NKJV), so *think big*. Remember, you can never outdo God.
- **Make marks on paper for a sense of control and freedom.** It's time for you to make your mark in this world. When you create something on your own, you will feel liberated and in control of your life. Make your mark, and make it grand.

7 The Importance of Play

"I had fun playing at work today," I exclaimed to an associate of mine. Not many adults can make this statement. All grown-ups do is "work, work, and work." They may play if they take vacations, but mostly they work. Toddlers play all day, with a few naps in between playtimes. Playing is how we learn. Through interacting with others, we increase our social and emotional skills. We practice such professional managerial traits as collaborating, leading, sharing, and encouraging others.

Toddler classrooms are equipped with

various types of manipulatives, toys, and figurines to engage play. This chapter will list a few practical toys that you need in your life as an adult to help you play.

Puzzles

As we discussed in chapter 3, puzzles help develop hand-eye coordination and fine motor skills. Toddlers learn how to twist, flip, and coordinate shapes. Too often our adult lives may seem like a big puzzle. As we try to figure it all out, it seems as if things are twisted, flipped, and not coordinated with our desired plans. The most important hint my mother gave me about puzzles is to look closely at the picture on the box before starting, and when you get stuck, look at it again. When was the last time you looked in the mirror? When your life seems flipped upside down, look in the mirror; you may have forgotten who you are as one of God's children. You are the head and not the tail. You are above and not beneath. Your life is not a puzzle. You just got stuck. Pick up the manual, the written word of God, and remind yourself of the picture He set before us—that when we're lost, all we have to do is look to the hills, which is where our help comes from.

Push-and-Pull Toys

These classic toys encourage toddlers to practice balance and coordination; they help children learn how to walk. They usually light up and have noisy movable parts. Toddlers pull up on these toys to help themselves stand after they've fallen. When toddlers are ready to walk, they push the toys. Within a few days, their success with the toys allows them to walk without holding on to anything.

As we grow older, we no longer need anything to help us walk, but we sometimes need a push-and-pull person to pick us up and remind us how to walk. Your push-and-pull adult should be a good friend who will stand in front of you and help lift you off the floor when you fall and will push you and pull you until you're walking on your own. In armed forces boot camps, the recruits usually practice climbing over a wall as a teamwork drill. This activity is not the easiest to complete alone. Teammates help push and lift one another over the wall, but most importantly, each person reaches back to lift the person who helped him over.

Who is pushing you? Whether it's a spouse, sibling, parent, friend, or mentor, be a good teammate by making sure you reach back to pull that person over when it's her turn. Great friendships form when each party grows from the other. If you're always doing the pushing and even the pulling sometimes, you may feel rejected, resentful, abandoned, or unappreciated.

Don't be the victim or the doormat or the project-based friend who creates every friendship in the interest of helping someone. You will deplete all you had available to pour in, leaving nothing to pour into yourself.

But don't be so independent as to

think you don't need anyone or anything but a rope — another option for cadets — to get over the wall. The rope has nothing to do with teamwork; it is used for one solitary purpose. It doesn't give anything back except blisters. Meanwhile the person coming behind you may need a helping hand in order to get over the wall. Don't be selfish. Offer your many gifts and talents to the person waiting for you to reach back. Get yourself a push-and-pull friend today. This person will bring balance and help coordinate your life. A push-and- pull friend is sure to change your life.

> *Get yourself a push-pull friend. It will change your life.*

Blocks and Building Sets

These are toys that spark the imagination.

Do you know what the favorite block activity of a toddler is? Newly enrolled toddlers at our childcare center would always venture to the bin full of colorful blocks sitting so brightly on the shelves. Without fail the first thing the child would do was pick up the entire colorful bin and pour all the blocks over the floor. Children also liked stacking the big, soft blocks to their height and then knocking them down. Then their imaginations would grow, and they would get the grand idea to make the towers taller for a more dramatic effect. Often teachers would have to limit the height of the towers to keep the children safe from the blocks plummeting over. And no matter how many times a tower fell or was knocked down by a classmate or the toddler himself, the toddler would eagerly rebuild the structure.

What's the lesson here? Learn how to knock down the towers in your life and build new ones. It may seem very challenging to enter a new situation, but don't be dismayed. You have been placed there as the response to the situation. Use your God-given skills to knock down barriers.

For example, when I became the

childcare director, many holes, gaps, and challenging towers stood before me. Initially, I tried to maintain the inherited structure, but it was against my nature. Minute by minute and hour by hour, I knocked down old mind-sets and created new ones. I hired a new staff to meet my standards, and we created a new culture in the building.

I encourage you to do the same. If your home is poorly assembled, then tear down what doesn't work and design a new home; and I mean that also for your internal structure. If you're in a new job and the previous person left without training you, learn as best and as fast as you can and then create your system. Don't get too upset when you mess up. Sometimes toddlers work hard on building their structures and then accidentally bump them, causing them to fall. They become very angry and have meltdowns. The teachers coach them not to worry and just to rebuild their towers. After a few tears, they do, and sometimes other toddlers even offer to help them. "If at first you don't succeed, try, try again."

I'm reminded that a giant named Goliath was feared by an entire town — except for one brave shepherd who made Goliath fall with a slingshot and one smooth stone. Use what you have to knock down what's blocking you. Hey, you might even enjoy it, just as the toddlers did.

Toddler Living Tips:

- **Promote your social and emotional skills through play.** If you observe a toddler or preschool classroom, you might say the children play all day rather than learn. However, we learn by playing. And most importantly, we learn how to communicate with others through play. Sometimes as adults we work too much and communicate only by answering phones at our jobs or speaking to the few individuals in nearby cubicles. But when you play, you laugh and share your feelings and personality. Take yourself out of the corporate bag to engage a little; socialize with others and be open to feeling happiness in the comfort of others. Next time they ask you to join the team for lunch or weekend golfing, go ahead and play with them.

- **Promote your imagination through dramatic play.** In the dramatic-play area, the toddlers became whomever they imitated. They were astronauts, parents, police officers, race car drivers, or construction workers. Using their imaginations, they built skyscrapers and demolished towers. You haven't lost your imagination; you just forget to think outside the box to create new and different things sometimes. Take the time to build your dreams by reconstructing your plans; exploring your options; and trying something new at your job, in your home, or in your leisure activities. You might find yourself earning a promotion or developing a favorite pastime.
- **Make playdates.** They're important. Early friendships are made on playdates and in preschool. I loved seeing the kids run into the classrooms to hug their favorite playmates. It made their mornings to see their friends. But when we grow older, if we experience a sour relationship or a

series of them, we sometimes vow never to have another girlfriend or best buddy ever again. But the Bible says in Ecclesiastes 4:9–10 NKJV, "Two are better than one, because they have a good reward for their labor. For if they fall, one will lift up his companion." Remember: a push-and-pull friend helps you get up and encourages you to keep going. Don't become an island unto yourself; extend yourself on a playdate, and have some fun with your friends.

8 Whom Are You Mimicking?

The most popular activity center, especially for girls, in a preschool classroom is the dramatic-play area. The dramatic-play area engages children in mimicking their adult caregivers. The area is often a small representation of a familiar home environment, consisting of a refrigerator, stove, sink, baby beds, sofas, and miniature laundry machines. Teachers also add career clothes like a doctor's white coat and hat, a police vest and hat, high heels, and men's shoes. Boys and girls pretend to be adults.

They naturally mimic their parents or other loved ones they see daily. Even though most of the toddlers have only a three-to-five-word-sentence vocabulary, their body language and few plain words exemplify adult behavior from their perspectives. One day a parent stopped in my office to inquire if any of the teachers put their cell phones in their bras. As she and I chuckled, she told me that her eighteen-month-old daughter, while playing at home, was pulling blocks out of her shirt and saying, "Hello?" The mom assured me that her daughter was not imitating her. When I asked the infant/toddler teacher about it, she also laughed and confessed that she had pulled her phone out of her bra after putting the children down for their naps, unaware that the children were studying her moves to practice later.

In the movie *Concussion*, which stars Will Smith as a Nigerian forensic pathologist, the forensic pathologist advises his love interest that in America you must become the best version of yourself, and if you're unsure of who that is, you pick someone to impersonate and be the best version of that. I'm not advising you to steal someone's identity, nor am I saying you should pretend to be someone you're not. Proverbs 23:7 NKJV says it correctly: "As he thinks in his heart, so is he," which means you are who you think you are. If your thoughts of yourself are small, you will act accordingly. And we all tend to practice behaviors we are surrounded by (hence the reason for skinny jeans in an obese nation). So whom are you mimicking?

Take an inventory of your friendships and surroundings. If you are the most intelligent person in your group, then you need to make some new friends and keep growing. If your clique consists of people who are always struggling, don't be surprised if you start to struggle. Remember the phrases "birds of a feather flock together" and "guilt by association." The assumption of these phrases is that we accompany people with whom we have commonalities in personality. What I like about the statement

Will Smith's character makes is the part about being the best versions of ourselves. Toddlers have nailed it; when they pretend to be adults, they confidently embody grown-up personas.

Scripture tells us in 1 Peter 2:9 NKJV, "But you are a chosen generation, a royal priesthood, a holy nation, His special people, that you may proclaim the praise of Him who called you out of darkness into His marvelous light." This scripture affirms that you are chosen, you are royal, you are special to the Almighty God, and you must know and understand your greatness. You don't just have the potential, kid; you have the whole package of excellence. The famous "What would Jesus do?" bracelet encourages us to act better, do better, and be better — basically to imitate Jesus. As we used to say, "You better check yourself." Review your actions. Review your last employment evaluation. If

> *You don't just have the potential, kid; you have the whole package of excellence.*

it contained anything about how to improve your behavior, make sure you work on those attributes if you want to keep your job. If you're friendless, you may want to become friendlier. Be the best version of yourself because God created only one you with distinct DNA and fingerprints. So go ahead and make your mark in the world; we await the phenomenal you.

Toddler Living Tip:

Be a little imitator. Who is your role model? Connect with someone who is doing what you desire to do in a few years — maybe invite the person to lunch — and ask him or her to be your mentor. We all need someone to push us.

9 Go Ahead: I Dare You To *Jump*!

During a visit to a family member's home, I vividly and authentically saw the meaning of the word *jump*. We were sitting in the kitchen and family room talking among ourselves, and in ran our rambunctious two-year-old, who stole the spotlight as he was placed on the island to share with the family another fascinating dance he had quickly learned. As we all smiled and laughed, in walked his favorite teenage uncle. While the busy toddler was still standing on the island, his uncle played with him fearlessly as all the nurturing women in the kitchen watched carefully, making sure the toddler didn't fall.

As his uncle pretended to walk away, he said to his nephew, "*Jump!*"

Without hesitation, without any fear, with only trust, and with his uncle about two feet away, the young explorer jumped into his uncle's arms—perfect catch! They laughed hysterically as the bodacious child begged to "do it again."

This was not the first time I had witnessed a toddler's faithful leap. I had seen it often between father and son. Yet learning how to lift the body off the ground doesn't come easily for toddlers. At first practice, they barely get their feet off the ground, only moving the top halves of their bodies back and forth in preparation to leap. Then, after they eagerly practice lifting their feet while standing, they lift one foot at a time, like they are marching, and thrust their stomachs, hoping to get both feet off the ground, until they have full ability to jump. In my toddler class, girls and boys practiced their jumping skills by jumping off first one step and then two, and it seemed as if the boys' initiation into preschool age was to daringly leap from higher than two steps.

Let's review the term *jump* as defined on the Dictionary.com website. *Jump* is an action verb that can have any of the following meanings:

> 1. To spring clear of the ground or other support by a sudden muscular effort; leap
>
> 2. To rise suddenly or quickly
>
> 3. To move or jerk suddenly, as from surprise or shock
>
> 4. To obey quickly and energetically; hustle

Notice all the action that takes place in this four-letter word. There is leaping, rising, obeying, and hustling. Also note the adverbs *suddenly*, *quickly*, and *energetically*. These terms indicate that a sense of urgency is needed, which means no procrastination — no putting off things until tomorrow — and no delay.

Through the jumping demonstration by

the abovementioned toddler who courageously sprang off the counter, God showed me the meaning of trust: confident reliance on someone. So let me illustrate the scene in this way: Think of your career. Are you planning to leave your job to seek a new job or even start your own business? Have fear, intimidation, hesitation, procrastination, or reservations held you back? Well, as with the two-year-old jumping off the counter, the time has come for you to understand that God has placed you upon a pedestal. Placed on a higher platform, you have an aerial view of your current circumstances and can see beyond today to what's absolutely possible. Before you look, though, I caution you that you may not want to return to your current circumstances. Look out and see past the forty-plus hours of your workweek, during which you have to answer to someone else. Stop quarreling with yourself. As Abram told his cousin Lot, stop all the quarreling and look at what God has given you (Genesis 13:8 MSG). It's plusher beyond your nine-to-five with a 401(k) (which may not be there tomorrow). There may be a business venture that you and your best friend, colleague, or family member have been talking about for the past few years but have yet to make a serious move toward. You may want to write a short story, travel the world, dance, or become a full-time musician. Has your mind begun to race with ideas? Great, now you're getting the gumption to climb onto the counter. You are suddenly rising.

So why do we jump, anyway? Have you ever seen kids leap into the pool or off the landing of a staircase? One of the first things they do is take a good look at their landing destination. They usually do not leave the platform until they trust the situation to "catch" them. In this instance, I'm saying seek God, find Him, learn how to trust Him, and let Him be your guide and direct your path. Once He gives you your instructions to your destined place, don't forget the last definition given for *jump*: "to obey quickly and energetically." Be obedient to all that God reveals and teaches you to do; it will be time to hustle.

Let's get back to the kids at the side of the pool or top of the stairs. The next thing they do—after they have evaluated the risk and their confidence is secure in the person or the situation below—is take a few steps back to gather momentum. Taking a few steps back on this occasion does not equate to the phrase "two steps forward and five steps back." Backward steps in this case are giving you a moment to prepare yourself for greatness and to fly. "Backward" steps for those seeking a new business may be working on a business plan and eliminating some existing debt by cutting back on spending habits. For those who are planning to travel, the steps may be to review finances and obtain or update a passport. Those who are seeking a new job might polish up their resumes and start dressing for the position they desire. Yes, that may mean no more business casual khaki pants and shirts but instead wearing a button-down shirt with a tie or a beautiful dress or suit and heels. Dress as if you want to be the CEO. Those who are in love and would like to marry could start preparing their minds for being with one person.

Allow me to share my jumping experience with you. I had worked at a nonprofit organization for eight years, when I'd started that job, I'd told myself I'd stay there less than ten years.. After four years as the youth coordinator, I accepted the promotion to the challenging position of childcare director. I set goals for the program and myself. Each goal caused a different "death in my flesh" by challenging my abilities, will, and emotions as I learned how to strengthen my business, management, and administration skills.

As I pressed toward the mark, my performance and efforts caused my supervisor to take notice. During my annual evaluation, the CEO noted my high performance and said that the time had come for me to advance my career by pursuing my personal goals. She was aware of my desire to work in a school and was pulling me out of my comfort zone. She was willing me to try something new that had been burning in my spirit. I was shocked and amazed that she saw beneath my day-to-day skills to my authentic talent.

I knew then that God was shifting me. So like many others, I looked for another job: my "dream job." I went back to school, made the necessary connections, and applied to multiple organizations. You're probably expecting me to say that I got the job right away. Nope! It was another year before I moved from my position. But during that year, while I kept getting rejected because of too much or not enough experience, I evaluated my master plan of having my own business. I created vision boards, conducted meetings with programs whose philosophies matched my own, and hired someone to hold me accountable and make sure I accomplished my goals of starting my own business. And as I developed this newfound zeal, the old position became stale, and even the allure of the "dream job" had faded.

Something happened one February day when I pulled into my job's parking lot and gathered my belongings to go in and start another day. As I climbed out of my car,

I looked at the doors of my precious childcare center, and a tear dropped as my mouth opened to say, "I don't want to be here anymore." Shocked by this, I pushed my way through as much as I could, and by the end of the day, I knew I was getting pushed out of the nest because it was very uncomfortable. I informed my CEO that this was the year I would be leaving but that I did not yet know the exact time.

I wish I could say I had everything lined up when the day did arrive, but I didn't. Despite what our elders taught us, I didn't have another job waiting for me, I didn't have six months to a year of rent saved up, and I didn't know if anyone would hire me as his or her consultant. What I did was prepare myself as much as possible. I eliminated some spending, paid my rent for a few months, and promoted myself as a consultant by sending out folders with proposals of my business. I continued to interview for different positions, and by the end of July, I jumped out of my childcare position.

And within one month of being off, I received a call asking me if I would consider being a consultant for a program. He caught me! The position came at a perfect time, as I had secured my bills, savings, and rent for only one more month. So when my new supervisor said, "I want to make sure you're paid for the upcoming pay period rather than keeping you in the hole," my spirit leaped again because I knew my bank account contained enough to sustain me for only one more month. All bills were due after the fifteenth. My salary increased from what it had been at the childcare center, I paid all my bills, and I even had a chance to travel to Canada for vacation. He caught me.

As you are preparing to launch, you are like the rock that will be catapulted from the king's slingshot. God is getting you ready to kill your giant! Take a few steps back, and gather your momentum to run and *jump*! For when you jump, you shall land in the safety of His arms, which are willing to catch you.

Many people use God as an excuse for why they haven't stepped out on faith to move toward what He has called them to do. For example, friends or relatives may explain their procrastination and failure to complete goals as the results of God's delay in connecting them with the resources. They may say, "As soon as God can bless me with a car, I can get my dream job," when in fact, they can get to those jobs by using public transportation. Once they make the initial move, God may move and bless them with their cars.

How can people use God as an excuse not to go forward? You may be waiting on God, but God is waiting for you with open arms:

> Trust GOD from the bottom of your heart; don't try to figure out everything on your own. Listen to God's voice in everything you do, everywhere you go; He is the one who will keep you on

track. Don't assume that you know it all. Run to GOD! Run from evil! Your body will glow with health; your very bones will vibrate with life! Honor GOD with everything you own; give Him the first and the best. Your barns will burst, your wine vats will brim over (Proverbs 3:5–12 MSG).

I triple-dog dare you to jump!

Toddler Living Tip:

Open the Door. The last stage of toddlerhood is when a child turns three years old (thirty-six months). By then, toddlers have lived in this massive universe for a short time, but they have learned much. During this last stage, they will utilize all of those foundational skills they've acquired on their way to preschool. They can now walk upstairs using alternating feet. They can stand briefly on one leg. In the summer months, they can finally ride those tricycles that were purchased thirty-five months earlier. They have increased verbal skills and a better command of the language for better communication with others. Likewise, now that you have built your coordination and balance, can verbalize your wants and desires, have attempted something new, and have learned to jump, you have reached the end of toddlerhood and can now open doors. May the doors to your genuine heart's desire open to you in your exploratory toddler-like life.

Toddler Living Tips

Chapter 1: Curious

- **Create expeditions out of normality.** In your normal daily tasks, take a moment to ask yourself, "What do I really want to do and why haven't I done it yet?" Each day try to explore something new such as taking a different route to work, eating at a new restaurant for lunch, or visiting a place you have wondered about for the past few months. This is your moment to explore your surroundings. When you travel to a new city or country, plan to have a new experience, such as cooking, dancing, swimming, or sightseeing, or even jump into a big sink hole. Don't just visit familiar places and eat at the same restaurants that you have in your town; explore something new.
- **Ask questions.** I hear educators say, you can always tell how intelligent someone is by the questions they ask. Toddlers are known for asking "why" all the time. Instead of just accepting

the status quo, inquire how to change your circumstances. You are a child of God and do not have to settle for mediocrity.

Chapter 2: Know That *No* Means *NO*

- **No is a sentence.** One year my mom told us that during the week of Thanksgiving she was practicing using the word no. Her birthday usually falls during that holiday week, therefore she gave her disclaimer in advance that she would be using her authoritative no. And as the cooking and clean up chores came about, when we asked mom to help she smiled while simply using her one word sentence, "*no*". You'll be surprised how liberating it is to say no and how much time you regain when kindly declining someone's request. And remember no is a sentence; there's no explanation needed.
- **Be steadfast and unmovable.** The Bible says in 1 Corinthians 15:58 MSG, "With all this going for us, my dear, dear friends, stand your ground. And don't hold back. Throw yourselves into the work of the Master, confident

that nothing you do for him is a waste of time or effort." Toddlers are very confident in their decisions. This is the reason you see little girls wearing princess dresses mixed match shoes and boys wearing superhero costumes in the grocery stores because they won the fight with their parents to dress in their favorite outfits. Practice assertiveness and confidence, and try to avoid arrogance.

- **Do something different from what you are asked to do.** Have you ever witnessed someone tell a toddler to do something and they immediately respond with no and do the opposite thing they were instructed not to do? For example, a parent tells the child to stop running and they keep running, or the parent asks the child to kiss them and the child turns their head. I always appreciated my staff who would exceed my expectations by enhancing the directive I gave them. Dare to go beyond other people's expectations of you. Surprise them by exerting effort to do things a little differently. Remember that raises and promotions are often given to those who take initiative to enhance their work performance.

Chapter 3: Independently Dependent

- **Exercise your independence.** During this stage, toddlers learn to dress themselves, zip a zipper, and manipulate figures. Just as they learn new skills, you can learn something new, like dance, a new language, or how to pay your own bills.
- **Feed yourself.** If you attend church, this is a great time for you to learn how to encourage yourself. Although your pastors and church leaders are there for you, you have to start feeding yourself with the Word of God to increase your faith muscles.

Chapter 4: Time for a Temper Tantrum

- **Be aggressive and take it by force.** When toddlers have a temper tantrum because someone took away their toy, they are known to grab the toy back from the person who took it from them. What has the enemy stolen from you? Get upset and go get your stuff! "For the kingdom suffers violence, and the violent take it by force" Matthew

11:12 NKJV.
- **Become frustrated when things don't go your way.** Go hard after what you want, whether it's a date, partner, job, car, home, or promotion. Make something happen; don't settle.
- **Learn how to throw and kick.** Find out how to throw away things that you don't need and that are holding you back. Kick out all of those negative things, people, and habits that hinder your development.
- **Ask for items by name.** Be specific in your requests to receive the true desires of your heart.

Chapter 5: Exploration Try

- **Try new things.** Doctors often advise parents to allow their toddlers to try new foods, toys, and places. My advice to you is the same. Venture out of your comfort zone. New opportunities don't usually knock on your door; you have to seek new activities, new jobs, new friends, and even new talents. Pick up a pencil to draw something; you might discover that you are an artist.

Chapter 6: Use Large Paper and Crayons

- **Make marks with crayon on paper or the table.** Make some marks to create your vision. Set aside time to envision the big dream. You don't have to wait to retire or earn more money; plan your future today. Why put things off until tomorrow? Have an arts and crafts day, a business-writing day, or a vision board day. "He encourages us that He will do exceedingly, abundantly, above what we ask or

think" (Ephesians 3:20 NKJV), so *think big*. Remember, you can never outdo God.
- **Make marks on paper for a sense of control and freedom.** It's time for you to make your mark in this world. When you create something on your own, you will feel liberated and in control of your life. Make your mark, and make it grand.

Chapter 7: The Importance of Play

- **Promote your social and emotional skills through play**. If you observe a toddler or preschool classroom, you might say the children play all day rather than learn. However, we learn by playing. And most importantly, we learn how to communicate with others through play. Sometimes as adults we work too much and communicate only by answering phones at our jobs or speaking to the few individuals in nearby cubicles. But when you play, you laugh and share your feelings and personality. Take yourself out of the corporate bag to engage a little; socialize with others and be open to

feeling happiness in the comfort of others. Next time they ask you to join the team for happy hour or weekend golfing, go ahead and play with them.
- **Promote your imagination through dramatic play.** In the dramatic-play area, the toddlers became whomever they imitated. They were astronauts, parents, police officers, race car drivers, or construction workers. Using their imaginations, they built skyscrapers and demolished towers. You haven't lost your imagination; you just forget to think outside the box to create new and different things sometimes. Take the time to build your dreams by reconstructing your plans; exploring your options; and trying something new at your job, in your home, or in your leisure activities. You might find yourself earning a promotion or developing a favorite pastime.
- **Make playdates.** They're important. Early friendships are made on playdates and in preschool. I loved seeing the kids run into the classrooms to hug their favorite playmates. It made their mornings to see their friends. But when we grow older, if

we experience a sour relationship or a series of them, we sometimes vow never to have another girlfriend or best buddy ever again. But the Bible says in Ecclesiastes 4:9–10 (NKJV), "Two are better than one, because they have a good reward for their labor. For if they fall, one will lift up his companion." Remember: a push-and-pull friend helps you get up and encourages you to keep going. Don't become an island unto yourself; extend yourself on a playdate, and have some fun with your friends.

Chapter 8: Whom Are You Mimicking?

- **Toddlers are little imitators.** Who is your role model? Connect with someone who is doing what you desire to do in a few years—maybe invite the person to lunch—and ask him or her to be your mentor. We all need someone to push us.

Chapter 9: Go Ahead: I Dare You to *Jump*!

- **Open the door.** The last stage of toddlerhood is when a child turns three years old (thirty-six months). By then, toddlers have lived in this massive universe for a short time, but they have learned much. During this last stage, they will utilize all of those foundational skills they've acquired on their way to preschool. They can now walk upstairs using alternating feet. They can stand briefly on one leg. In the summer months, they can finally ride those tricycles purchased thirty-five months earlier. They have increased verbal skills and a better command of the language for better communication with others. Likewise, now that you have built your coordination and balance, can verbalize your wants and desires, have attempted something new, and have learned to jump, you have reached the end of toddlerhood and can now open doors. May the doors to your genuine heart's desire open to you in your exploratory toddler-like life.

References

Beldan, A. C., N. Thomson, and L. Luby. 2008. "Temper Tantrums in Healthy Versus Depressed and Disruptive Preschoolers: Defining Tantrum Behaviors Associated with Clinical Problems." *The Journal of Pediatrics* 152 (1): 117–22. doi:org/10.1016/j.jpeds.2007.06.030.

Leshkovska, E. A., and S.M. Spaseva. 2016. "John Dewey's Educational Theory and Educational Implications of Howard Gardner's Multiple Intelligences Theory." *International Journal of Cognitive Research in Science, Engineering and Education (IJCRSEE)* 4 (2): 57–66. doi:10.5937/IJCRSEE1602057A.

Li, L., G. Quinones, and A. Ridgway. 2016. "Noisy Neighbours: A Construction of Collective Knowledge in Toddlers' Shared Play Space." *Australasian Journal of Early Childhood* 41 (4): 64–71.

McCarty, M. E., R. K. Clifton, D. H. Ashmead, P. Lee, and N. Goubet. 2001. "How Infants Use Vision for Grasping Objects." *Child Development* 72 (4): 973–87. doi:10.1111/1467-8624.00329.

Niolon, R. 2003. "House Tree Person Drawings." Intelligentietesten. http://www.intelligentietesten.com/house_tree_person_drawings.htm.

Taylor, E. 2008. "Providing Developmentally Based Care for Preschoolers." *AORN Journal* 88 (2): 267.

Scripture References

1 Corinthians 15:58 (MSG): With all this going for us, my dear, dear friends, stand your ground. And don't hold back. Throw yourselves into the work of the Master, confident that nothing you do for him is a waste of time or effort.

1 John 4:4 (NKJV): You are of God, little children, and have overcome them, because He who is in you is greater than he who is in the world.

1 Peter 2:9 (NKJV): But you are a chosen generation, a royal priesthood, a holy nation, His own special people, that you may proclaim the praises of Him who called you out of darkness into His marvelous light.

Matthew 7:7 (NKJV): Ask, and you shall receive; seek, and you shall find; knock, and the door shall be opened.

Ephesians 3:20 (NKJV): Now to Him who is able to do exceedingly abundantly above all that we ask or think, according to the power that works in us.

Habakkuk 2:2-3 (MSG): And then God answered: "Write this. Write what you see. Write it out in big block letters so that it can be read on the run. This vision-message is a witness pointing to what's coming. It aches for the coming—it can hardly wait! And it doesn't lie. If it seems slow in coming, wait. It's on its way. It will come right on time."

James 1:2-4 (MSG): My brethren, count it all joy when you fall into various trials, knowing that the testing of your faith produces patience. But let patience have its perfect work, that you may be perfect and complete, lacking nothing.

James 1:5–8 (MSG): If you don't know what you're doing, pray to the Father. He loves to help. You'll get his help, and won't be condescended to when you ask for it. Ask boldly, believingly, without a second thought. People who "worry their prayers" are like wind-whipped waves. Don't think you're going to get anything from the Master that way, adrift at sea, keeping all your options open.

Jeremiah 33:1–3 (MSG): Moreover the word of the Lord came to Jeremiah a second time, while he was still shut up in the court of the prison, saying, "Thus says the Lord who made it, the Lord who formed it to establish it (the Lord *is* His name): 'Call to Me, and I will answer you, and show you great and mighty things, which you do not know.'"

Proverbs 3:5–12 (MSG): Trust God from the bottom of your heart; don't try to figure out everything on your own. Listen for God's voice in everything you do, everywhere you go; he's the one who will keep you on track. Don't assume that you know it all. Run to God! Run from evil! Your body will glow with health, your very bones will vibrate with life! Honor God with everything you own; give him the first and the best. Your barns will burst, your wine vats will brim over. But don't, dear friend, resent God's discipline; don't sulk under his loving correction. It's the child he loves that God corrects; a father's delight is behind all this.

Genesis 13:8 (MSG): Abram said to Lot, "Let's not have fighting between us, between your shepherds and my shepherds. After all, we're family. Look around. Isn't there plenty of land out there? Let's separate. If you go left, I'll go right; if you go right, I'll go left."

ABOUT THE AUTHOR

TATIANA WELLS, has a MA in Early Childhood Education and a background in child care and development including experience as a child care director, 4th grade assistant teacher and youth and family coordinator. As a PhD candidate, Tatiana seeks to impact education to ensure families and children are exposed to quality opportunities to enjoy the fullness of life with joy. Tatiana is also a faithful member of her church serving as the praise dance leader and intercessor. She also mentors youth and young adults motivating them to pursue all that God has for them by embracing their God-given talents and abilities.

www.ingramcontent.com/pod-product-compliance
Lightning Source LLC
LaVergne TN
LVHW051507070426
835507LV00022B/2978

www.ingramcontent.com/pod-product-compliance
Lightning Source LLC
LaVergne TN
LVHW051507070426
835507LV00022B/2978